ORLAND PARK PUBLIC LIBRARY

3 1315 00516 9151

S0-AAC-081

DEC   2009

DISCARD

ORLAND PARK PUBLIC LIBRARY
14921 RAVINIA AVENUE
ORLAND PARK, ILLINOIS 60462
708-428-5100

Families and their Faiths

Hinduism in Bali

Written by Frances Hawker and Putu Resi
Photography by Bruce Campbell

Crabtree Publishing Company
www.crabtreebooks.com

ORLAND PARK PUBLIC LIBRARY

j294.5/HAW

Crabtree Publishing Company
www.crabtreebooks.com

Authors: Frances Hawker
and Putu Resi
Editors: Su Swallow and
Lynn Peppas
Proofreader: Crystal Sikkens
Editorial director: Kathy Middleton
Designer: Robert Walster, Big Blu Design
Photographs: Bruce Campbell
Artwork: Ketut Suardana
Production coordinator: Katherine Berti
Prepress technicians: Margaret Amy Salter
and Katherine Berti

Frances Hawker and Bruce Campbell have traveled all around the world, beginning when they made their way overland from Europe to Australia thirty-five years ago. They have previously published ten children's books together.

Putu Resi acted as coordinator, translator, and adviser on the cultural aspects of the book. She is the keeper of a temple at Sindhu beach in Sanur, Bali, and is greatly involved with dance performances.

Library and Archives Canada Cataloguing in Publication

Hawker, Frances
   Hinduism in Bali / Frances Hawker and Putu Resi ;
photography by Bruce Campbell.

(Families and their faiths)
Includes index.
ISBN 978-0-7787-5008-6 (bound).--ISBN 978-0-7787-5025-3 (pbk.)

   1. Hinduism--Indonesia--Bali Island--Customs and
practices--Juvenile literature. 2. Bali Island (Indonesia)--
Religious life and customs--Juvenile literature.
I. Campbell, Bruce, 1950- II. Resi, Putu III. Title. IV. Series:
Hawker, Frances. Families and their faiths.

BL1163.8.B34H39 2009   j294.509598'62   C2009-902110-2

Library of Congress Cataloging-in-Publication Data

Hawker, Frances.
   Hinduism in Bali / written by Frances Hawker and Putu Resi ;
photography by Bruce Campbell.
       p. cm. -- (Families and their faiths)
   Includes index.
   ISBN 978-0-7787-5025-3 (pbk. : alk. paper)
-- ISBN 978-0-7787-5008-6 (reinforced library binding : alk. paper)
   1. Hinduism--Indonesia--Bali Island--Customs and practices--
Juvenile literature. 2. Hindus--Indonesia--Bali Island--Social life
and customs--Juvenile literature. I. Resi, Putu. II. Campbell,
Bruce, 1950- III. Title. IV. Series.

   BL1163.8.B34H38 2009
   294.509598'62--dc22

                                        2009014297

Crabtree Publishing Company

www.crabtreebooks.com
1-800-387-7650

Published in Canada
Crabtree Publishing
616 Welland Ave.
St. Catharines, ON
L2M 5V6

Published in the United States
Crabtree Publishing
PMB16A
350 Fifth Ave., Suite 3308
New York, NY 10118

Published by CRABTREE PUBLISHING COMPANY
Copyright © 2010 All rights reserved. No part of this
publication may be reproduced, stored in a retrieval system
or be transmitted in any form or by any means, electronic,
mechanical, photocopying, recording, or otherwise, without
the prior written permission of Crabtree Publishing Company.

Published by Cherrytree Books (a member of the Evans Publishing
Group) Copyright © in the text Frances Hawker 2009. Copyright
© in the photographs Bruce Campbell 2009. This edition published
under licence from Cherrytree Books. All rights reserved.

Contents

This is a story about my granddaughter, Yoni. I have ten grandchildren. Yoni is the youngest. She is seven years old. We live on the small island of Bali, in Indonesia.

Here we are dressed up for a special ceremony at the temple.

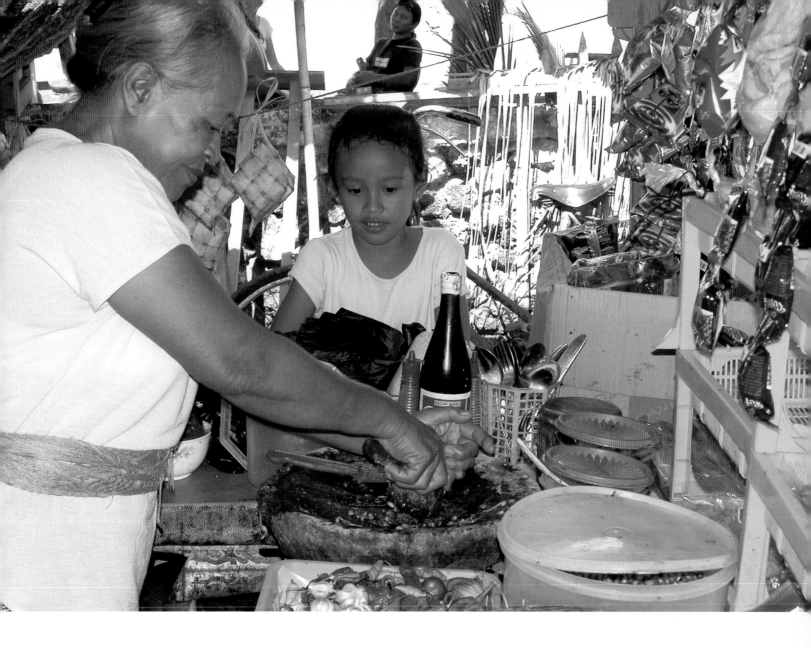

    I run a small café on the beach. It is called
a **warung**. People come to my café while the
children play and swim in the sea.

    Yoni likes to watch me cook. The people
of Bali like hot, spicy food. I grind the spices
and hot chilies with a stone.

Yoni wakes up early each morning to go to school. School starts at 7:30 AM, and finishes at 10:00 AM. Yoni is in class one, and there are 40 children in her class.

Every morning the children pray to the goddess of learning, Saraswati, to help them at school.

6

In the afternoons Yoni likes to swim with her friends. There is a calm **lagoon** in front of our house. Yoni's uncle, Made, likes to fish with his net. He catches small fish in the shallow water for us to eat for dinner.

Yoni's great-grandfather makes musical instruments for the **gamelan** orchestra. He uses **spells and chants** to give them a magical sound.

Yoni wants to learn to play.

8

Like most Balinese we are **Hindus**.

Dancing is very important to our religion or faith. Yoni and her friends have dance lessons. Before their lessons they go to the temple to thank the gods for the gift of dancing.

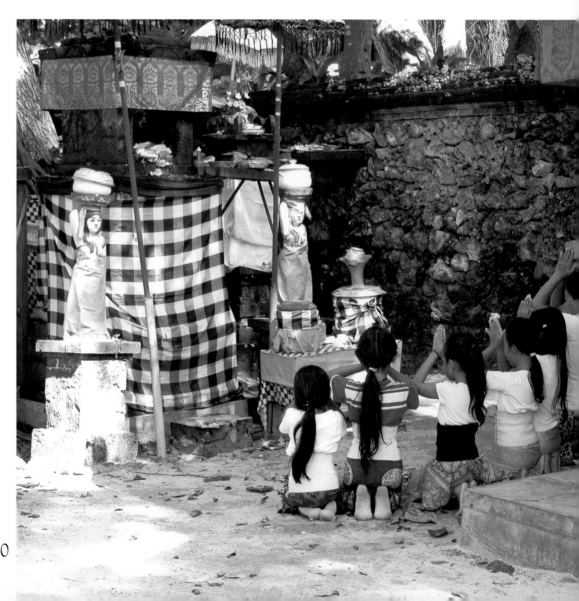

I help Yoni make **offerings** for the gods. We fold coconut leaves into boxes and fill them with flowers. There are red petals for Brahma, white petals for Shiva, and green leaves for Wisnu.

We light **incense** sticks so the smoke carries our prayers and gifts up to the gods.

11

We give small offerings several times each day. Women put them in the family temples and around the house. Bus drivers put them at crossroads, where spirits meet. Musicians place them on their instruments.

We make larger offerings for ceremonies. We take piles of rice cakes and fruit to the temple. A priest blesses them.

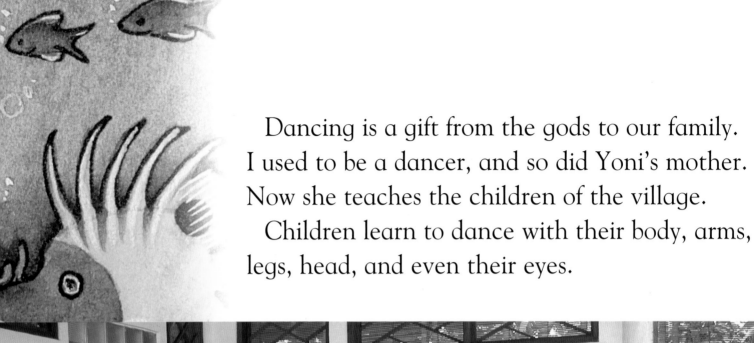

Dancing is a gift from the gods to our family.
I used to be a dancer, and so did Yoni's mother.
Now she teaches the children of the village.
Children learn to dance with their body, arms,
legs, head, and even their eyes.

The girls giggle as they get ready to dance at my warung. Tourists and local people come to enjoy the dance and the music.

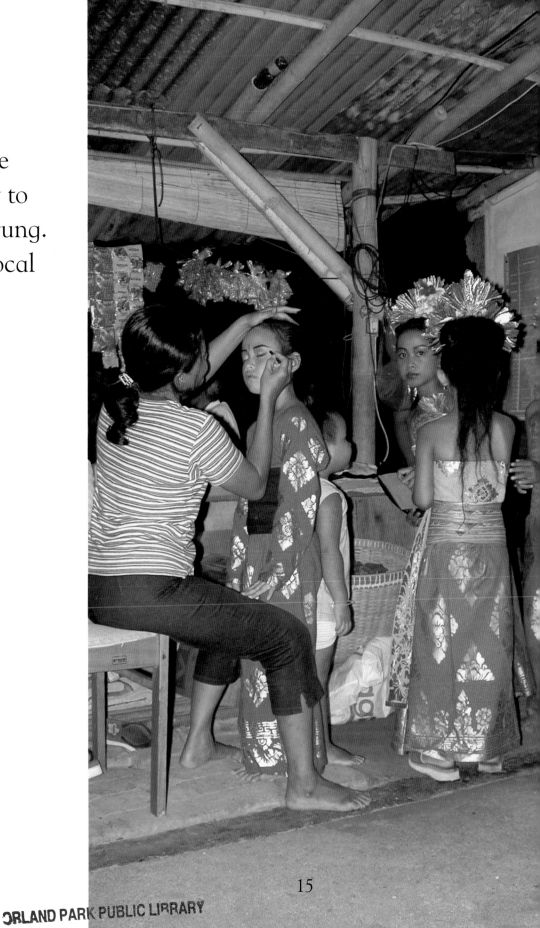

15

ORLAND PARK PUBLIC LIBRARY

Many of our dances tell stories. Some of the stories come from a famous Hindu story called the **Ramayana**.

In this dance Yoni shakes the trees and collects the most perfect flowers that fall to the ground. She makes these into a beautiful **headdress** for a princess.

16

Here Yoni is a bird trying to protect the queen. The dance is very long. Yoni has to remember every flick of the eyes, every twist of the fingers, and every turn of the toes.

18

Yoni practices for a special ceremony at the temple. She practices the dance over and over for weeks. She will not stop until it is perfect.

On the day of the ceremony Yoni wakes up early. She is very excited. Yoni's mother dresses her to look beautiful as she dances for the gods. She wraps her in eight meters of gold printed material. Then she winds a yellow cloth around her waist. Finally, she places a crown with gold, jewels, and flowers on her head.

We all dress up for the ceremony. It is to bless and **purify** the temple. We know that our gods and the spirits of our **ancestors** will come for the celebrations and prayers. Everything must be perfect.

Yoni is worried about the dance. What if she forgets something?

Yoni watches as a priest blesses the
other little dancers. Their costumes
glisten in the sunlight.

They dance to welcome the visiting
spirits. The temple has no roof so that
we can be linked to the gods above.
We can hear the priests chanting.

23

Suddenly there is a loud clanging from the gamelan orchestra. A boy dancer leaps on to the floor. He looks fierce in his ancient warrior's costume. On his back he wears a **dagger** that has magical powers. He is the guardian of the visiting spirits. He spins and stamps and charges. The music plays louder and louder, faster and faster, until the warrior's dance suddenly ends.

The dance is just too scary for little Wayan.
She starts to cry, and the girls comfort her.

26

The time has come for Yoni to dance.
I pray to the gods that she will dance
beautifully. The men in the gamelan
orchestra can sense the power of the
dance. They play better than ever.

There is a hush in the crowd. Everyone can feel the magic. Yoni has been blessed with *taksu*. The spirit of the dance has entered into her and is dancing with her.

28

The gods are happy with our little dancer.
And so are we.

Notes for parents and teachers

Hinduism began in India at least 5,000 years ago. It is the world's oldest religion, and has approximately a billion followers, mainly in India and Nepal. Hindus believe that everything comes from an eternal spirit called Brahman, the source of all life. Hindus worship many gods and goddesses. Three of the most important are Brahma, Wisnu, and Shiva.

Balinese Hinduism is a fusion of different traditions. Balinese culture is rich and the people follow the traditions passed down from their ancestors. Bali is full of things you cannot see: gods, goddesses, good spirits, demons, bad spirits, prayers, spells, and magic.

Hindus believe in *samsara*. They believe that this life is just one of many that they experience. If someone leads a good life, their next one will be better. If they live a bad life, their next one will be worse.

Hindus believe that they are reincarnated. When they die they are born again in a new body to lead another life. If someone finally leads a perfect life, then they may get off the wheel of reincarnation and achieve a perfect state called *moksa*.

Page 6

Each child in Yoni's school must help clean the school when they arrive. They have their own broom and must help sweep the room and the outside area, wipe down the desks and, once a week, clean the windows.

Yoni's lessons finish at ten o'clock in the morning, and at 11 o'clock another year one class arrives and uses the same room.

Pages 8 and 9

Usually only boys and men play in gamelan orchestras. The bronze keys of the instruments make a wonderful, clear sound when they are hit with a wooden hammer.

There is no written music for these instruments. Small boys sit on their fathers' laps and learn by listening and watching over and over at ceremonies and practices.

Pages 11, 12, and 13

Offerings are given to spirits and ancestors, as well as gods. They are treated with great respect (see notes to page 22). Balinese give offerings not only to good spirits, but to bad ones too, to keep them happy.

Offerings need to be beautiful and are made from things the gods have given to people in nature, such as flowers, fruit, and leaves. These are given back to the gods as thanks. Small offerings include whole flowers or petals, cut fruit, and chopped pandanus leaves.

Large offerings that are taken to the temple are blessed by a priest, and then carried home on women's heads and eaten. They can include flowers, fruit, rice cakes, and decorations made from woven palm fronds. Sometimes people can place whole roast piglets on the offerings.

Pages 14 and 15

Dancing really does run in Yoni's family. Her great-grandfather was a dancer who danced at temple festivals. Her grandmother was a *janger* dancer and danced and sang in a group of five girls and five boys. Although Yoni is only seven years old she is already a talented dancer. She has won many dance competitions that are run between different villages. She has also won a prize for the best little dancer in Bali on Balinese television.

Pages 16 and 17

The *Ramayana* is an epic poem, which tells the story of Rama and his wife, Sita. It has 24,000 verses, and is thought to have been composed some 5000 years ago. The poem forms part of the Hindu scriptures.

Page 22

During this ceremony gods and ancestors visit their worshipers and relatives. Temples in Bali are in simple open courtyards where people can communicate directly with their gods.

Page 23

These dancers are called *rejang dewa* dancers. They welcome and entertain the visiting spirits. This is a sacred dance and can only be danced at religious ceremonies.

Glossary

ancestor A relative who died a long time ago
dagger A short knife
gamelan A group of musical instruments from Indonesia
headdress Decorated covering for the head
Hindu A person who follows the religion of Hinduism
incense Something that is burned to make a pleasant smell
lagoon A calm area of sea, protected by a reef
offering A gift given to the gods to thank them or ask for help
purify To clean something thoroughly
Ramayana A long poem telling the story of Rama and Sita. It is part of the Hindu scriptures
spells and chants Words and songs that some people believe have magical powers
taksu A performance that is guided by the gods
warung The Indonesian name for a café

Index

ORLAND PARK PUBLIC LIBRARY

Printed in China—CT